# Exploring
# Celtic Britain

# Exploring
# Celtic Britain

## DENISE STOBIE

COLLINS & BROWN

First published in Great Britain in 1999
by Collins & Brown Ltd
London House
Great Eastern Wharf
Parkgate Road
London SW11 4NQ

British Library Cataloguing-in-Publication Data:
A catalogue record for this book is available from the British Library.


ISBN 1-85585-687-5 (hb)


1 3 5 7 9 8 6 4 2


Creative director: Julian Holland
Designed by Nigel White
Origination by Colour Symphony, Singapore
Printed in Hong Kong by Hong Kong Graphic & Printing Ltd.

**Photographic Acknowledgements:**
Sarah Boait: p.74
Simant Bostock: p.23(t), p.78/79, p.98/99, p.100/101
Hamish Brown: p.80, p.81, p.82, p.88/89, p.90, p.92, p.93
Historic Scotland: p.94/95, p.96/97
Julian Holland: p.5, p.28/29, p.30, p.31, p.32, p.33, p.34
Peat Moors Visitor Centre: p.14/15, p.16, p.17, p.18, p.19, p.20, p.21
Royal Commission on the Ancient & Historical Monuments of Wales: p.45, p.47, p.54/55, p.57, p.59
Denise Stobie: p.26/27, p.35
Ivan Stobie: Half-title page, p.77, p.83, p.84, p.85, p.86, p.87, p.91, p.102/103, p.104/105, p.106/107,
p.108/109, p.110, p.111
David Titchener: Front cover, Back cover, Title page, p.8, p.10/11, p.12/13, p.22, p.23(b), p.24, p.25, p.36, p.37,
p.38, p.39, p.40, p.41, p.42/43, p.44, p.46, p.48, p.49, p.50, p.51, p.52/53, p.56, p.57(inset), p.58, p.60, p.61,
p.62, p.63, p.64, p.65, p.66, p.67, p.68, p.69, p.70/71, p.72/73, p.75

Front Cover: *St Govan's Chapel, Pembrokeshire, where it is said that the cliff steps cannot be counted*
Back cover: *12th century Dolbadarn Castle, built by the Welsh to resist the English*
Half-title page: *A reconstructed Romano-Celtic tombstone outside
the temple at Vindolanda Roman fort, on Hadrian's Wall*
Title page: *Tre'r Ceiri hillfort on the Lleyn Peninsula in Wales*
Contents page: *Maiden Castle hillfort, Dorset, with the most impressive ramparts in Britain*

# CONTENTS

| | | | |
|---|---|---|---|
| 1 | Mousa Broch | 29 | Dinas Emrys Hillfort |
| 2 | Broch of Gurness | 30 | Ffynon Gybi |
| 3 | Sueno's Stone | 31 | Tomen-y-Mur Roman Fort |
| 4 | Dun Torcuill | 32 | Nevern |
| 5 | Dun Telve | 33 | St Govan's Head & Chapel |
| 6 | Iona | 34 | Carew Cross |
| 7 | Dunnichen Stone | 35 | Carmarthen |
| 8 | Roughcastle Roman Fort | 36 | Castell Carreg Cennen |
| 9 | Lindisfarne | 37 | Kilpeck Church |
| 10 | Bamburgh | 38 | Caerleon |
| 11 | St Ninian's Chapel | 39 | Caerwent |
| 12 | St Ninian's Cave | 40 | Peat Moors Visitor Centre, Westhay |
| 13 | Vindolanda Roman Fort | 41 | Glastonbury |
| 14 | Chesters Roman Fort | 42 | South Cadbury Hillfort |
| 15 | Jarrow, St Paul's Church | 43 | Maiden Castle Hillfort |
| 16 | Monkwearmouth, St Peter's Church | 44 | St Cleer Holy Well |
| 17 | Durham | 45 | King Doniert Stone |
| 18 | St Winifred's Well, Holywell | 46 | St Neot |
| 19 | Maen Achwyfan Cross | 47 | Castle Dore |
| 20 | Din Lligwy Hut Circles | 48 | St Michael's Mount |
| 21 | Caer Gybi | 49 | Carn Euny Village & Wells |
| 22 | Holyhead Mountain Hut Circles | 50 | St Buryan Crosses |
| 23 | Menai Strait & Anglesey | 51 | Alsia Holy Well |
| 24 | Bardsey Island (Ynys Enlli) | 52 | Kenidjack Castle, Promontory Fort |
| 25 | Carn Fadryn Hillfort | 53 | Madron Holy Well |
| 26 | Tre'r Ceir Hillfort | 54 | St Piran's Cross |
| 27 | Caernarfon | 55 | The Rumps Promontory Fort, Pentire Head |
| 28 | Ffynon Beris | 56 | Tintagel |

## INTRODUCTION

THIS BOOK defines Celtic Britain in terms of its geography rather than its history. Those areas of our island which never quite succumbed to conquest or invasion, which retained a uniqueness and a nationality all of their own with only a surface gloss of Roman–ness or Englishness – those are the places I have chosen. I have had to be selective, and I have tried not to be predictable. The west country, Wales and Scotland are the relevant areas, with northern England added for good measure. The sites chosen are among the most beautiful in the country, and all of them could be visited by the public at the time of writing. Each site has an Ordnance Survey Grid Reference, and there is a map at the beginning of the book to guide you around the countryside. But where is Celtic Britain, and what can be found there?

'Iron Age' and 'Celtic' Britain are terms often used interchangeably. The culture which can be traced in the British Isles between about 600BC and the Roman invasion in AD43 was in a direct progression from the Neolithic and Bronze Ages, but the art of smelting iron in Britain coincided with an influx of ideas and peoples from the continent which we now describe as 'Celtic'. Whether the Celts invaded en masse or more gradually over several centuries, we cannot now determine.

The best evidence of the Iron Age in Britain is of settlement types. This rather dry archaeological term refers to the different types of farmstead, village, hillfort, and building which have been excavated and interpreted so that we can get some idea of how the Celtic people spent their lives. There are other forms of dwelling and settlement which can still be seen in today's western landscape: brochs, which seem to be peculiar to western Scotland; crannogs, which are artificial islands built in lakes and are most common in Ireland and Scotland, though one or two can still be seen in Wales; and courtyard houses, found in both Cornwall and Wales.

It is hillforts which are arguably the most spectacular Celtic remains still visible in the British countryside. They are by no means restricted to those geographical areas now considered to be 'Celtic', although forts (or hill top sites, perhaps a more accurate term) in the west of Britain still tend to be among the best preserved. Hilltop fortification can be as early as the new Stone Age, as excavations showed at South Cadbury in Somerset, but the multiple banks and ditches (ramparts) most often associated with this type of

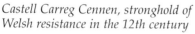

*Castell Carreg Cennen, stronghold of Welsh resistance in the 12th century*

site are usually from about the 2nd century BC. Some were places of permanent occupation, and were described by the Romans as 'oppida', a type of town. More were places of temporary occupation, perhaps refuges in times of war and raiding, or meeting places for trade or worship. It is virtually impossible to sum up these visually stunning places: I strongly advise that you visit at least one hillfort in your lifetime, as photographs can never do them justice.

The full flowering of the independent British Celts ended in 43AD. Schoolbook history starts with the Romans. If the native British are mentioned at all, the descriptions tend to fit the Stone Age – cave dwellers, dressed in skins, using flint or crude wooden tools. And then, suddenly, the Romans arrive and drag these primitive barbarians kicking and screaming into the civilised world. I have seen history books still in use which seem to ignore 1000 years of progress, in order to prove the glory of Rome compared with the savagery of the ancient Britons. The Roman invasion and conquest of Britain ensured that true, unadulterated Celtic culture ceased to exist on this island, although the western areas were less influenced than lowland Britain. If one follows the line of the Fosse Way from Exeter, north through Bath and Cirencester to Lincoln, then as Ermine Street north again to York, one can see a division between two lands which never truly altered. South and east of the line was the Civil Zone referred to in traditional history, which classicists would have us believe applied to the whole island: the upper strata of Celtic society adopted the customs, law, fashion, language, education and social order of their conquerors. Although remnants of Celtic culture survived, particularly in religion and art, within a century it was almost totally subsumed within the richer, more luxurious lifestyle espoused by the new order. However, many native homesteads remained virtually untouched by Roman lifestyle for the entirety of the occupation.

North and west of the boundary was known as the Military Zone. Few towns and villas here: in Cornwall, most of Wales, and virtually all of Scotland, the British were not conquered. They were contained. I believe that on the whole, the British tribes in the military areas adopted only those few aspects of Roman culture which suited them, and rejected others as being irrelevant. Culture here was much more 'Brito–Roman' than 'Romano–British'. To what extent they abandoned their British–ness and aped their masters is not known. Exploring this area now, it is as though the land watched, traded with and used the foreign invader, then quietly absorbed all traces back into the granite, as though it had never been.

I have been challenged for including so many Roman sites in a book supposedly on Celtic Britain, but I believe that after 43AD the Celts can only truly be recognised in terms of their resistance to outsiders – first the Romans, then the Saxons, and the Normans, and the English. It is in the areas where the would–be conquerors were forced to build their strongest defences that the Celtic spirit of freedom can most readily be appreciated, and it is those defences which survive today. Additionally, the settlements which arose around Roman defences were wholly native, and so represent the Celtic people during Roman rule.

The withdrawal of Roman troops in 401 marked the end of an era. By 409, Britain was beset on all sides by invaders: Irish in the west, Picts to the north and Saxons in the east. An appeal to Rome for military aid was met with the terse reply: 'Look to your own defences'. Britain reverted with gratifying swiftness to its pre–Roman Celtic tribal structure – unfortunately, it also reverted to its Celtic feuds and inter–clan warfare. Britain needed to protect itself from foreign invasion, but who was going to tell the clans that they must fight together to retain their homeland?

This period is known as the Dark Ages and is inextricably linked with the great hero Arthur. Never a king but certainly a brilliant soldier, it was he (or someone like him) who stopped the British people from being immediately overrun by new conquerors. Other names from the period, such as Vortigern, Ambrosius, Merlin and Lancelot – all of them known only in legend and with no historical authentication whatsoever – crop up where we know the British resisted the new invaders with all the skill they possessed. This skill seems to have been based on Roman military patterns but with an overlay of decidedly Celtic pride. The list of Arthur's '12 Battles' gives us the occasional location, but these are based more on guesswork than fact. Iron Age hillforts were refortified during the foreign invasions, perhaps because the technique of building in stone had been lost in the chaos of the Roman withdrawal, or even beforehand as the Empire declined. We know that many Roman administrative centres were no longer being maintained in the classical manner, and many command posts were being rebuilt in timber before 400. The Celts used their old skills to fortify places they could defend, rather than rely on crumbling masonry for protection.

Lowland Britain was swiftly settled by Anglo–Saxon incomers. By the middle of the 6th century, the development of 'England' was well underway. But Devon held out against Anglicisation until 710, and Cornwall until 825. There are still Cornish natives who believe England begins 'over the Tamar', and does not include the western peninsula. Most of Wales and Scotland never had the pleasure of greeting the Saxon invaders at all, although they did have Irish settlement to contend with, notably in the south–west of both lands.

And it was the Irish, in the shape of Christian holy men, who gave the west of Britain another purely, uniquely Celtic layer, for the Dark Ages and after were also known as the Age of Saints.

By the time the Romans left Britain, Christianity was the official religion of the island, and it is generally assumed that Arthur and his contemporaries were Christians. However, with the influx of pagan settlers, many natives reverted to the religions of their ancestors, and still others had never embraced the eastern faith in the first place. The structure of the Roman church was designed by an urban culture, and this did not sit well with the much more loosely organised Celtic society. The Irish, who had never felt the influence of urbanisation, felt much more at home with the concept of small monastic communities headed by an abbot – a small family unit, as it were – than with dioceses and bishops. Added to this idea, which had come to Ireland (and Wales) from Syria and Egypt via Gaul, was the tradition of hermits living alone in the wilderness, rejecting all worldly comfort in order to purify the soul. Some Celts embraced this idea wholeheartedly, believing that they should take the word of God to the people but hold no possessions of their own, not even a home. British Celts, fleeing to Ireland from the Saxon invasions, seem to have adopted this form of Christianity, and brought it back to their homeland. The monastic and eremitic traditions were particularly popular in Cornwall and Wales.

The saints were holy men and women who were known for their gentleness and Christian passion, as well as their ability to perform miracles. They were probably also revered for their wisdom, and sought out for judgements and mediation. They were granted lands by kings and chieftains. The similarity of their treatment and status to that offered to the druids cannot be denied, and in all probability the saints filled the void left by druidism.

It is impossible to detail all of the Celtic Christian sites in the west of Britain, so I have chosen a selection of the most typical. Wells and springs now with

*The plunge pool at St Winifred's Well in north Wales, where pilgrims immerse themselves in the healing waters*

10

saintly dedications were most likely held sacred long before Christ was born; some saints' names are simply rationalisations of pagan deities or even placenames, such as St Dennis which is a corruption of 'dinas' or fort. Celtic crosses were probably preaching stones, marking the spot where the missionary would preach to the people in the absence of a church, or even standing stones Christianised by the addition of a cross head. To find evidence of the Celtic saints in Cornwall, seek out any parish or village with a saint name – there are thousands to choose from. In Wales, those places whose names begin with 'Llan' usually indicate a sacred enclosure, with the second element of the name being that of the saint. Northern England and Scotland were almost wholly converted to Christianity by Irish missionaries such as Ninian and Columba, and their missions were accurately recorded by contemporary historians. The Christian sites of the north, therefore, are quite specific.

I have said little, if anything, about Celtic Britain after the Age of Celtic Saints. The Synod of Whitby in 664 marked the end of the Celtic Church, and after this hermits became fewer and liturgy was all Roman Catholic, controlled from Canterbury rather than St David's or Iona. One can recognise crosses and inscribed stones which are purely Celtic in nature right up to the 11th century, but the Norman Conquest, like all the other conquests before it, hammered another nail in the coffin of the Celts.

The Normans built castles all along the Welsh border, and the land became known as the Welsh Marches. Although a succession of Welsh princes resisted with all their power – the Celts again defined by those they fought – eventually they were subdued in the thirteenth century and Edward I built the mighty Welsh castles we recognise today. A measure of revenge was taken with the accession of Henry VII in 1485 (Tudor being a Welsh name, Tewdwr) but Wales became part of a United Kingdom in 1543. The Scots, now Irish speaking and, nominally at least, a single kingdom of Picts and Celts, held out a little longer. William Wallace, immortalised in the film 'Braveheart', eventually lost to English might, but Robert the Bruce drove the Sassenach back beyond the borders. A Scottish king, James VI, came to the English throne in 1603 and the countries were supposedly united, but it was in 1746 that the battle of Culloden marked the final stand of the Celtic kingdoms against the English. The Celts lost, and retribution meant that the last vestiges of the old tribal system, the Highland clans, were wiped out forever. Celtic Britain was no more. Long live the United Kingdom.

And yet . . .

While I was researching this book, the Welsh and the Scottish people voted in favour of their own assemblies. Soon Scotland will have its own parliament to go with its separate education and legal systems, still different from the English. Wales will have an assembly to legislate on Welsh matters. The Stone of Scone, the ancient Pictish coronation stone stolen from them by Edward I, has been returned to Scottish soil with an acknowledgement of wrongs done, and the Lindisfarne Gospels, written and illuminated in the Celtic style by British monks in an Irish–founded monastery, are to be returned to the north where they belong. Children in Cornwall can take an examination in Cornish, a British language thought to be dead. The Celtic spirit of freedom is far from dead. Those people who believed it was need only to travel into the west to see how it has continued unabated for almost three millennia.

DENISE STOBIE *GLASTONBURY 1998.*

*Defensive earthworks built across the 'neck' of Pentire Head, Cornwall*

# 1. THE WEST COUNTRY

THERE ARE HUNDREDS of prehistoric remains in Cornwall and the west country, and the reader is recommended to buy one of the many excellent guidebooks available in order to make a selection to visit. By the time the Celts were fully established as the dominant culture in this area, the local tribes were the Dobunni (Avon and north Somerset), the Durotriges (Wiltshire, Somerset and Dorset) and the Dumnonii (Devon and Cornwall). Cornwall was still called Dumnonia in Arthurian and Saxon times.

When the Roman hierarchy turned its sights westward in 44AD, General Vespasian led his troops into the lands of the Durotriges, where we are told that the Legio II Augusta 'fought thirty battles, conquered two powerful tribes and brought more than twenty oppida [towns]...under Roman rule' (Suetonius). Maiden Castle may have been one of the 20 oppida. Considering how quickly the occupying armies moved into the lands of the Durotriges and Dumnonii, there is remarkably little to show for their trouble. The western peninsula was not militarized, and those small villas which have been found might well have belonged to native Dumnonians who simply liked the architecture of the places they'd seen further east, over the Tamar. Isca Dumnoniorum (Exeter) marked the western limit of town building. The territory was not completely ignored, although much of the evidence we have is from the mid–3rd century. Coins, milestones and tin objects show two aspects of Celtic and Roman interaction: trade and roadbuilding. The first probably led to the second.

The west country is probably best known as the home of 'King' Arthur: Tintagel was said to be his birthplace and he is frequently linked with the armies of Dumnonia. Several hillforts in the area have Arthurian links, perhaps the best known being South Cadbury.

There are hundreds of sites linked with Celtic saints, such as wells, crosses and churches. Again, there are many excellent books on the subject and they are well worth reading if more information is required.

First, I would like to show a reconstructed 'typical' British settlement, so that we can get some idea of what time–eroded archaeological remains do not reveal. The value of such reconstructions is immeasurable in bringing the past to life, and I cannot imagine writing a book which begins in the pre–Roman Iron Age without showing the reader how these people might have lived.

*Peat Moors Visitor Centre, Somerset. Reconstruction of an Iron Age roundhouse*

### THE PEAT MOORS VISITOR CENTRE, WESTHAY

THE PEAT MOORS VISITOR CENTRE in Westhay (ST 427414), near Glastonbury, houses a museum and reconstructed buildings and artifacts based on information from Iron Age archaeology. Regular displays of ancient crafts are held there throughout the year, and the site wardens are extremely helpful in clarifying any information the visitor might require. These photographs illustrate, in a way words and excavations cannot, how life was for thousands of years of British history.

Houses in early Britain were almost invariably round. They varied in size from 3m (10ft) in diameter to upwards of 30m (98ft), and often contained a central hearth. The usual method of construction was to drive stakes into the ground at intervals to form a framework, then to weave supple withies through the stakes to form a wattle wall. This wall would then be covered, inside and out, with daub made from clay, dung and straw, which hardened to form a warm and weatherproof covering. Roofing methods varied; a framework of roof struts would be laid across the walls which would bear the weight and distribute it evenly, and then thatching material local to the area would be laid over this framework to form a steep, conical roof. Very large buildings

Left *The framework of a roundhouse, before the weatherproofing has been started*

Below *This reconstruction at the Peat Moors Visitor Centre in Westhay has a floor made of local clay*

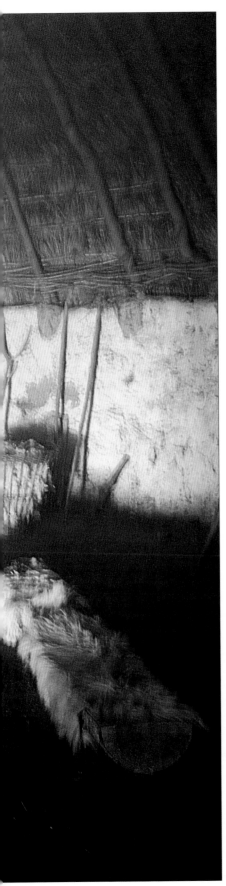

sometimes had a central roof post to support the weight. There are variations to this basic method, for instance a ring of thick posts may be driven in at intervals between the thinner stakes, thus providing extra support. A doorway, often with a roofed porch, would be provided to the building.

Sometimes the floor would remain beaten earth, although archaeological evidence for flooring is usually lacking. At the Glastonbury and Meare lake villages, on which the Peat Moors reconstructions are based, the floors were made of local clay which was brought in to the site before the houses were built. The wall stakes were then driven through both clay and the underlying soft ground, providing extra support.

Did they have windows? A race as intelligent and inventive as the Celts would surely have understood the concept of a window, but there is absolutely no evidence of this in the archaeological record. One can conjecture skylights in the thatching, but we will never know. (The word 'window' is Norse, and means 'wind–eye'. The Welsh for window, 'ffenest', is borrowed from Latin, implying that there was no early British equivalent.)

Most Celtic houses would have had a central hearth on which all meals would be cooked. There are many fine surviving cauldrons, cooking pots and 'fire–dogs' (across which a spit would be laid) which can be seen in museums across the country. At Glastonbury, where the underlying land was extremely soft, the weight of the hearth would cause the floor to sink and, eventually, the area would have to be levelled and a new hearth built.

Left *The interior has a central hearth, a bread oven and an upright loom for weaving cloth*

Below *These Soay sheep at the Peat Moors Visitors Centre are the closest surviving descendants of Iron Age sheep*

Some single buildings were found to have ten or more hearths overlying each other, as they were rebuilt over the duration of the house. Reconstruction shows that, although the lack of windows makes the houses slightly smoky, most of the smoke from the fire would fill the roof space and seep through the thatch. The soot and tar waterproofed the thatch, and the roof space made an ideal area for preserving meat and fish.

Animal bones found on the many excavated Iron Age settlement sites have told us not only the breeds of animal kept on early farms – mainly sheep, pigs and cattle – but also how these breeds were different to modern farm animals. Usually, they were smaller than those we see today. Cows were used for meat and leather, while pork seems to have been the favourite meat of the Celts. Often, burials have grave goods which include joints of pork. The sheep of the Iron Age were similar to these now kept at the Peat Moors Visitor Centre, and are a breed known as Soay. They are similar to goats in many respects. This breed has escaped much of the evolution of modern sheep because they were isolated on a Scottish island and have not been subject to intensive breeding programmes.

Most settlements were completely self–sufficient. This seems to have been the case regardless of the size of the settlement or the number of people who lived there. Virtually every house would have had its own upright loom for weaving cloth. The Celts were known for their brightly checked clothes, so it is safe to say that dyeing wool would also have taken place close to the dwelling. Crops of wheat, barley, peas, beans and other legumes would have been grown nearby, and tests have shown that these crops would have had a very high yield, providing plenty of food for the families.

Other crafts practiced routinely would have been pottery, woodworking and metalworking. Forges for working iron and bronze would have been in separate buildings. Pottery for everyday use was usually made in the settlement, although many larger sites show evidence of trade with other places and sometimes pottery from overseas, particularly the Mediterranean. A pole lathe was used for turning wood, and it is thought that the Celts were among the first people to practise 'coopering' – the art of making items such as buckets and barrels out of wooden staves held together with wooden or metal hoops.

Left *These people are dressed in clothing based on archaeological finds and Roman documentation*

Right *A pole lathe, used for turning wood, whose design has barely changed in 2000 years*

## CHYSAUSTER & CARN EUNY

ALTHOUGH THE ROUNDHOUSE which was so typical of Celtic areas can be found in almost any type of settlement, they were not always made of the wattle–and–daub described earlier in this chapter. Cornwall has examples of stone built dwellings which do not seem to have been specifically defensive. The English Heritage maintained site at Chysauster (SW 472350, not pictured), near Penzance in Cornwall , is an excellent example.

So is the settlement at Carn Euny (SW 400289), 4 miles (6.5km) from Penzance, which seems to have been occupied for more than 800 years. The earliest buildings were of timber, but seem to have been replaced by stone huts some time in the 1st century BC, around the same time as

Chysauster was first settled. Carn Euny was occupied well into Roman times. It is best known for its well preserved underground fogou (pronounced foo–goo). This underground passage and chamber is similar to those structures known as souterrains in Scotland and Ireland, but their purpose remains unknown. The fogou at Carn Euny had its entrance in one of the buildings, and a gallery with its capstones still in place measures 1.83m (6ft) high and 1.53m (5ft) wide. The underground passage is about 20m (65ft) long, and there is another gallery at the end. Various suggestions for the use of fogous have been suggested over the years, including underground store houses, cattle sheds, hiding places and ritual enclosures. As a hiding place during times of attack, a fogou would in fact be very dangerous, as there is only one entrance and it would probably turn into a death trap. We will probably never know the true use of these peculiarly Celtic structures.

Nearby are two holy wells dedicated to St Euny. He is said to have been the brother of St Ia (who gave her name to St Ives) and his feast day is February 2nd, the same day as St Bridget and the pagan Celtic festival of Imbolc. The well was known for its healing properties, particularly against rickets, and the afflicted child or person would be passed 3 times widdershins (anti–clockwise) through the water and then 3 times in the same direction on the surrounding grass. Fortune–telling was another property of the wells, and pins or pebbles would be dropped into the water as the pertinent question was asked, the number of bubbles arising from the object giving the required answer.

Above *Remains of stone houses at Carn Euny, Cornwall*

Top right *This is one of the best surviving examples of a fogou (underground passage), at Carn Euny*

Bottom right *A holy well dedicated to St Euny, but probably sacred since prehistoric times*

## KENIDJACK CASTLE AND THE RUMPS

PROMONTORY FORTS, or cliff castles, abound on the western peninsula of Cornwall. These are built on headlands which jut out into the sea. The narrower the approach to the headland, the better: the sea provides protection on three sides, and defensive earthworks of bank and ditch type only need to be built across the neck of land leading to the fort.

Kenidjack Castle (SW 354327), on the far western tip of Cornwall near Land's End, is one such fort. The area is worth visiting for the profusion of prehistoric remains, some of them earlier than the scope of this book: Merry Maidens and Boscawen–Un stone circles; Carn Euny settlement, fogou and wells; and Carn Brea hillfort (not pictured). I am not certain whether the promontory is the same place as the Carn Kenidjack mentioned in C Straffon's book 'Pagan Cornwall – Land of the Goddess', which is said to make strange and ghostly noises when strong winds blow, but the whole area, steeped in history, is worth a visit just for the atmosphere.

Another excellent example of a Cornish promontory fort is The Rumps at Pentire Head ('pen' means 'head') (SW 934810). The earthworks here still look as though the land has been folded like a concertina, even though the defences are 2000 years old. Also worth visiting are Trevelgue Head, said to be the finest cliff castle in Cornwall, Gurnard's Head and Treren Dinas, the latter two having Arthurian associations.

Left *Kenidjack Castle, an impressive promontory fort in western Cornwall*

Below *Bank and ditch defences at The Rumps, Pentire Head, Cornwall*

## SOUTH CADBURY

SOUTH CADBURY (ST 628582) stands some 75m (246ft) above the surrounding countryside, and the entire hilltop is surrounded by defences. Originally occupied in Neolithic and Bronze Age times, when it had only one bank and ditch, it continued throughout the Iron Age as an important centre in the Somerset countryside. The 4 or 5 outer earthworks now visible appear to have been first built in around 150BC, but were repaired several times. The full extent of occupation on the hilltop is not yet known, as only part of the surface has been excavated. For many years, it was thought that South Cadbury was another casualty of the Roman campaign into the west country. Excavations found the remains of 30 men, women and children where they had been slaughtered on the road to the south west gateway, left where they fell to be mutilated by wolves and wild dogs. They were massacred with, it appears, little warning. Among their remains were scattered brooches and other wares which indicated that a market of some kind was taking place in the approach to the fort when the attack came. Careful analysis of the dating evidence, however, shows that this massacre – which ended tribal occupation at Cadbury forever – happened about 30 years later than Vespasian's campaign.

In the intervening generation, the inner rampart of the defences was rebuilt, the ditch cleaned and the bank raised. A Celtic temple inside the fort was probably used during this 30–year period, and the Roman pottery which was found is evidence of trade, not occupation. The massacre had nothing to do with the Boudiccan rebellion, because that was 10 years in the past. We have no idea why, after 3 decades of being left in peace to live in their hilltop home, the inhabitants were suddenly driven out or murdered. We do know that at this time, the village that is now South Cadbury was greatly enlarged, while other survivors may have been moved to nearby Catsgore or Ilchester (Lindinis).

It may be that the Cadbury dwellers posed a threat by their very existence, continuing with a way of life that the Romans wanted to eradicate. After all, free Celts were dangerous Celts.....

Cadbury was next occupied in the fifth century, and has in recent years become widely accepted as the home or headquarters of an 'Arthur–type figure'. The impressive hill was massively re–fortified by a person of great importance. The

*The south west gate at South Cadbury, where 30 skeletons were found by archaeologists*

building techniques used, particularly on the ramparts, virtually ignore 400 years of Roman architecture and hark back to the glory days of the late Iron Age. The buildings within the defences were rectangular rather than circular, but were of the familiar wattle–and–daub construction. Approaching the hilltop from the village of South Cadbury, the hedge–lined path leads to the remains of one of the lesser gateways. The opposite corner of the enclosure shows a wider but flatter gap: the main gate, which was once a two–storey square gateway with two sets of massive double doors.

The overall picture is one of restored Celtic pride. Fragments of pottery show that the inhabitants of the settlement were able to import luxury goods from the Mediterranean, like oil and wine.

*Cadbury Castle may have been King Arthur's Camelot in the 5th century*

## MAIDEN CASTLE

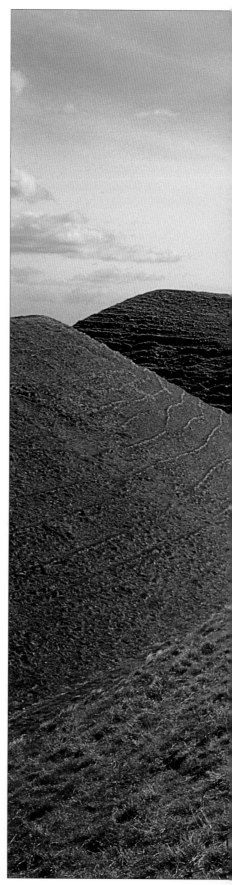

MAIDEN CASTLE (SY 670885) in Dorset is probably the best known and most impressive of all British hillforts. Like South Cadbury, it was first occupied in Neolithic times, and a longbarrow (prehistoric burial mound) was built here. The amazingly complex entrance earthworks, which seen from the air resemble a child's comic–book maze, can only be appreciated by a personal visit. It was probably the tribal capital of the Durotriges, who were famous for their artwork and pottery, and was one of the main targets of the Roman campaign of western suppression in 44AD. There seem to have been several artillery assaults, and some hand–to–hand fighting. Between assaults, the inhabitants had time to bury their dead in what pre–war archaeologist Sir Mortimer Wheeler described as a war cemetery, with some grave goods. Several skeletons found in the graves had sword cuts to the head, and one unfortunate was found with the head of a Roman ballista bolt still in his ribs. After the defeat, the population of Maiden Castle was resettled in purpose–built Durnovaria (Dorchester). Later in the Roman period, a Romano–Celtic temple was built on the summit of the fort, and coins and votive offerings have been found here. The foundations are still visible.

*Below and right* The massive earthworks at Maiden Castle, Dorset, which was the tribal capital of the Durotriges

## ST MICHAEL'S MOUNT

WE KNOW THAT, even before Rome laid its greedy hands on Britannia, there were trade links between Cornwall and the Mediterranean, most particularly in tin. What is strange is that, until about 250AD, most Roman tin came from Spain. Whatever the cause of this anomaly, after this date there is evidence that Cornwall became the major source of the metal for the Roman Empire. After mining and smelting, the tin was cast into ingots which were stockpiled at Ictis Insula – probably St Michael's Mount (SW 515298) which later became inextricably linked with Arthurian legend. From here, the precious metal was taken all over the known world.

*Below St Michael's Mount, Cornwall, was the Roman Ictis Insula where tin was stockpiled for export to the whole Empire*

## TINTAGEL

TINTAGEL CASTLE (SX 048892) rises some 250 ft/77m above the wild Atlantic coast of northern Cornwall. This promontory fort is the legendary birthplace of the Dark Age hero Arthur. The legends, mostly written down in medieval times, seize on Arthur as the hero who held back the barbarian advance of Picts, Irish, Angles and Saxons in the 5th century. History shows that he was ultimately unsuccessful, although the western Britons did halt the Saxon advance for almost 50 years.

Tintagel is now more an island than a promontory, reached by a somewhat precarious path. The castle remains on the island are of the thirteenth and fourteenth centuries, built on the foundations of a fortress a century older. Above the castle, extensive remains have been found of buildings from the fifth or sixth centuries – Arthur's time. For many decades, this was considered to be a Celtic monastery and thus discounted as a chieftain's stronghold. The current opinion is that these remains are the headquarters of a powerful British lord, and Tintagel could mark the re–emergence of a substantially British aristocracy.

Above *Tintagel Castle, Cornwall, home of a British chieftain in the time of Arthur*

## CASTLE DORE

ONE SUCH HILLFORT, with a legendary link to Arthur, is Castle Dore in Cornwall (SX 103548). It is a double–rampart hillfort, strategically placed on the ancient trade route across the Cornish peninsula, and was re–fortified during the fifth and sixth centuries. In legend, it is the home of King Mark of Cornwall, the old man in the Tristan and Yseult (or Isolde) stories. The ramparts still stand some 6–7ft/2m high. Excavations have uncovered the remains of two halls, one of which was much larger than the so–called palace at Cadbury, the other being approximately the same size. Not all of the interior has been excavated, nor has the outer gate which may well have been defended by a similar gatehouse to that found at Cadbury. A cobbled road led into the interior.

Recent work has caused doubt to be placed on the 'Arthurian' occupation of Castle Dore, but the tradition is firmly established.

*Right The remains of Glastonbury Abbey. King Arthur is said to have been buried here after the battle of Camlann*

*Below Castle Dore, Cornwall, an Iron Age hillfort which was reoccupied in Arthurian times*

## GLASTONBURY

MUCH OF OUR KNOWLEDGE and speculation about Dark Age history is triggered by the Arthurian legends, including an early medieval text listing 12 supposed battles. The most successful of these was at Mount Badon, thought to be Liddington hillfort (SU 208796, not pictured) in Wiltshire. Something must also be said about the warrior's death. His final battle was 'the strife of Camlann', and the British word used implies a skirmish rather than a full–scale battle. As is always the case, the location of this skirmish is not known, but it has been variously located in Cornwall (Slaughterbridge), Somerset (nr Cadbury), and on Hadrian's Wall near Birdoswald fort, which was called Camboglanna. The most firmly entrenched legend is that he was buried at Glastonbury Abbey (ST 501388) in Somerset, and in 1191 a coffin made of a hollowed–out oak tree was discovered in the Abbey graveyard. The monks made much of a lead cross supposedly buried with it, claiming that it was the grave of Arthur. Glastonbury has many myths of its own attached to it, most of them with some Celtic leaning, and its role in the Celtic Christian church was very important.

Legends abound in and about Glastonbury. The monastery ruins are medieval, but it is said that the original church was built by Christ himself, a tale which inspired William Blake's hymn 'Jerusalem'. The first church was built of wattles, and the earliest community was supposedly founded in 31 or 63AD by St Joseph of Arimathea, who brought with him the Holy Grail. Other Celtic saints linked with this holy ground include St Patrick who, on discovering a lonely community built on the Irish pattern, took it upon himself to restore it to order; St Bridget, who established a community of nuns at Beckery (Bec–Eriu, Little Ireland) about a mile west of the town where Bride's Mound can just about be seen; and Saints David, Gildas, Illtud and a host of others, all of whom lent their names to Glastonbury's immense medieval reputation.

### ALSIA HOLY WELL

ALSIA WELL (SW 394251) is on the furthest western peninsula of Cornwall, between St Buryan and Land's End. It has a reputation as a wishing well, but there is no building over the spring. Like many Cornish wells and springs, the most efficacious time for healing is the first three Wednesdays in May, and the well seems to have been best known for healing rickets in children. It has no specific associated saint, but St Buryan, after whom the parish is named, was said to be the beautiful virgin daughter of a Donegal king. She came to Britain with Saint Patrick, and was converted to Christianity by St Piran. It is interesting that her saint's day has fallen (at various times) between May 1 and June 4, bearing in mind the healing times ascribed to the well.

### ST CLEER WELL

THE WELL AT ST CLEER, near Liskeard (SX 249682), was used as a bowsenning well in past centuries. Bowsenning was a brutal form of shock treatment used on the 'insane' – those suffering from hysteria or epilepsy, for example. At Altarnun (SX 226816, not pictured), the well water ran into a walled pit, and the 'lunatic' was stood on the wall with his back to the water. Without warning, he was pushed into the water where an attendant would thoroughly and roughly immerse him, handling him like a bundle of dirty washing until the combination of cold water and violence calmed him down. He would then be taken to the church and prayed for. If the cure worked, then the saint was thanked; if not, the whole sorry process was repeated, according to a contemporary witness, 'againe and againe while there remained in him any hope of life for recovery'.

There is some doubt as to whether Cleer is a Celtic saint at all: the name could be a form of Clare and related to the religious order of the Poor Clares; or it could be a variation on

Left *This atmospheric well is at Alsia, Cornwall. Such wells were sacred to the Celts*

Below *St Cleer holy well, Cornwall. The cross is much older than the wellhouse*

Clarus or Claro, which is the dedication of the church. A cross, much older than the fabric of the well building, stands within the walled enclosure, but the wellhouse dates from the 15th century. The well itself probably pre–dates the 13th century church. It is said that stones taken from the well will mysteriously return of their own accord by dawn on the following day.

## MADRON WELL

MADRON WELL (SW 445328) is still a site of pilgrimage. The trees around the well are decorated with offerings to the saint – or spirit – of the well, either in thanks or hope for a cure. Ribbons, rags, even clothing, garland the well and continue a tradition which probably pre–dates the Celts themselves. The name of St Madron (also known as Maternus in Latin and Medhran in Irish) is said to be a corruption of Patern(us) or Madurn, a Breton priest–bishop who died in the mid 6th century. However, the association I make with the name is from the name of a Celtic deity known as 'Mabon ap Madron', sometimes translated as Sun, son of Mother. Thus, I would speculate that Madron is also the name of a Celtic mother–goddess, making the dedication of the well much earlier than is usually supposed.

## ST NEOT CHURCH WINDOW

THE RIGHT HAND PANEL of the Young Women's Window in St Neot Church (SX 188679) shows a man with many children held in his lap. Some experts believe it depicts God or Christ with the saints (or all of humanity) cradled in his arms. Others, however, say that the man is in fact St Brynach or Brychan, a Welsh king who gave his name to Brycheiniog in Wales and who is credited in Celtic Christian legend with the paternity of more than 20 Celtic saints. It is obvious from this tale, and others such as that of St Nun, mother of Welsh patron saint St David, that celibacy was not a prerequisite of the Celtic religious life.

Above *For 2000 years or more, pilgrims have left offerings at Madron Well in Cornwall*

Right *St Brynach, father of more than 20 saints, portrayed in stained glass at St Neot Church in Cornwall*

## ST PIRAN'S CROSS

PIRAN'S CROSS (SW 772564) can be found at Penhale sands, in Perran Bay just south of Newquay . This is an excellent example of a so–called 'Cornish' cross, with its round, pierced head and short side projections above the body of the pillar. It has been speculated that this style of cross pre–dates Christianity, and comparisons have been made with the shape of the Egyptian ankh. The cross marks the site of the buried oratory of St Piran, thought to be the earliest building of its kind in the west country. Legend has it that the church was part of the city of Langarrow, buried by sands in a storm which lasted 3 days. A second church was built inland, but this too was buried in the dunes. The church of St Piran in Perranzabuloe is the third to bear the name, and parts of its masonry were brought from the earlier buildings.

## ST BURYAN CROSSES

ONE OF THE CROSSES at St Buryan (SW 409258) seems to be a pre–Christian standing stone which has been sanctified by the addition of a wheel cross. It could be that many such crosses exist throughout Britain. It was an official policy of the church to give pagan sites Christian associations, in the hope that the local people would readily accept the change of allegiance. The churchyard at St Buryan has five such crosses, one at the head of each of the roads leading from the church.

## THE DONIERT STONE

FINALLY in this selection of West Country sites, I must mention the many memorial stones dating from the Christian period. A fine example is the Doniert Stone (SX 238689) which is located between St Cleer and Redgate Farm, beside the main Liskeard road. It appears to be a cross base, and its interlace patterns have been described as Hiberno–Saxon – Hibernia being the Latin name of Ireland. The inscription appears to commemorate a 9th century king Durngarth, who died in 875. It reads: DONIERT ROGAUIT PRO ANIMA (Doniert ordered this cross for the good of his soul).

Another stone worth seeing for its Arthurian associations is the Tristan Stone (SX 112521), which can be found beside the A3082 near Fowey.

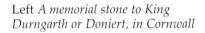

Far left *St Piran's cross, Penhale Sands, Cornwall, marks the site of the earliest church in the county*

Left *A memorial stone to King Durngarth or Doniert, in Cornwall*

Right *One of the crosses at St Buryan in Cornwall*

## 2. Wales

L IKE CORNWALL, the prehistoric remains which abound in the Welsh countryside are innumerable. The Celtic tribes of the country included the Demetae, Ordovices and Silures. Pre–Roman Wales is perhaps best known for being the cradle of Druidism. Their 'university' was on Anglesey, and it was said that Druidic training took 20 years, for nothing was ever written down and all facts were committed to memory. Apart from the later Christians, no other religious hierarchy so terrified the Roman administration as this class of priests, judges and lawgivers who held incredible political sway with the Celtic aristocracy. It is possible that they were, with their propaganda and absolute power, the greatest single threat to Roman conquest in the western empire.

Although we know of determined Roman military activity from both contemporary documents and archaeology, no permanent advances were achieved in Wales or Scotland until around 70–80AD. Probably the most famous Roman assault was that on Anglesey in 60–61AD when the Druids were attacked. It is likely that Anglesey would have suffered a full Roman occupation at this point, but for the fact that the armies of the Iceni, Parisi and Trinovantes (and probably others), led by the Icenian queen Boudicca, were in full rebellion in the south–east of Britain. Most remains of the Roman period are military in nature, showing that the Welsh tribes were not amenable to Roman occupation.

Even today, the inhabitants of this land are unwilling to give themselves the name 'Welsh', for to do so would be to call themselves foreigners in their own land. The word 'wales' was Saesneg (Saxon) for stranger or foreigner, so the term 'Cymru' is preferred. It was, however, a native chieftain who is blamed for bringing the Saxon hordes into Britain in the first place. Vortigern, whose fortress may have been on Dinas Emrys, is said to have invited Saxon warriors into Britain to fight the pagan hordes of Picts and Irish who were attacking various frontiers. In return, he gave them lands in Kent. After they had succeeded in their mission, he was unable to accede to their growing demands for land and fled back to his fortress. His successor, for whom Dinas Emrys is probably named, was Ambrosius Aurelianus, mythically the uncle of Arthur.

*Dolbadarn Castle (SH 588597) in Wales, begun by Llywelyn ap Iorwerth in the early 12th century. The round tower is unique in medieval Wales*

The sacred lands of many Celtic saints can be found in Wales, often prefixed by the word 'Llan'. It is possible that Celtic monasticism originated here, but the structure was refined in Ireland and brought back by missionaries. St David and St Illtyd, amongst others, are credited with founding some of the greatest Christian schools in the early Christian world, at Llantwit Major and Llancarfan.

Wales retained a system of close family or clan structure well into the Middle Ages, similar, it is believed, to pre–Roman tribal society. The endless incursions of the English, culminating in the castle building of the 13th and 14th centuries, however, eventually wore them down .

Above and Right *Holyhead Mountain Hut Circles, Anglesey, was a British settlement overlooking the Irish Sea*

## HOLYHEAD MOUNTAIN HUT CIRCLES

HOLYHEAD MOUNTAIN HUT CIRCLES (SH 212820), in the very west of Anglesey in N Wales, are an excellent example of stone built roundhouses. The remains are of some 20 or so buildings, although more than 50 were recorded in 1865. The site appears to have been occupied, like Chysauster in Cornwall, from the 1st century BC well into the Roman period. There are both circular and rectangular foundations, and deviation from the normal Celtic roundhouse pattern usually indicates distinct Roman influence. The use of stone rather than wood or wattle is also a useful pointer. The confirmation, however, comes from finds of pottery from the 3rd and 4th centuries. It is unclear whether stone formed the full height of the walls with thatching on top, or whether wattle–and–daub walls were raised on stone foundations. Some of the huts still have visible central hearths, and one of the rectangular huts shows evidence of copper working.

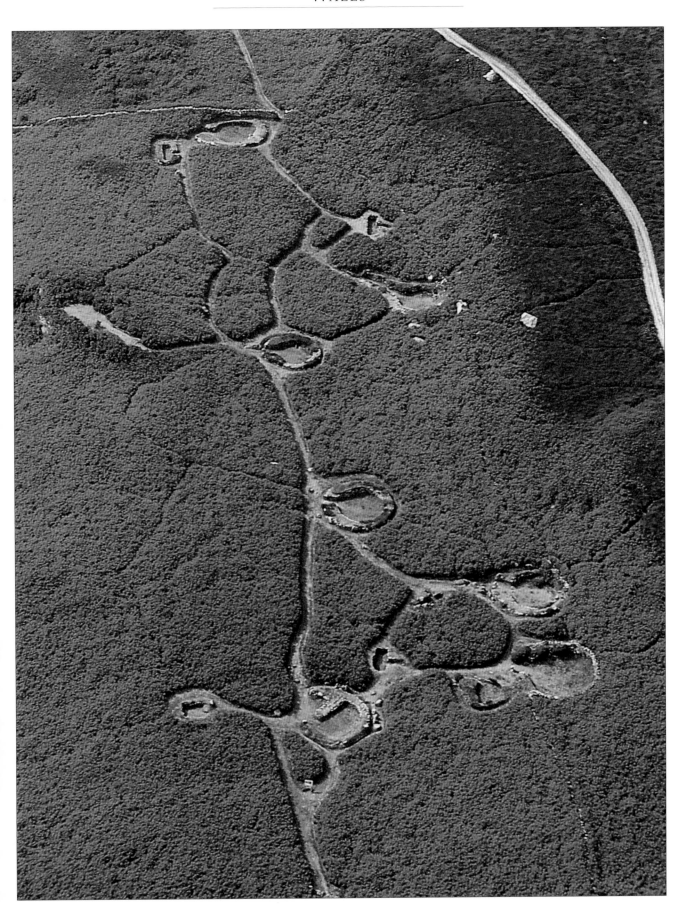

## TRE'R CEIRI & CARN FADRYN

FOR WILD LONELINESS, Tre'r Ceiri (SH 374447), on the Lleyn Peninsula in N Wales, can barely be matched. It was a pre–Roman stronghold of the Ordovices tribe, and the name means 'Town of the Giants'. A true hillfort, the settlement covers 2.2ha (5 acres) of a wild mountain top, surrounded by a stone wall which still stands up to 4.5m (15ft) high. There are the remains of some 150 huts, and by 1982 69 of them had been excavated. Although there were no exceptional finds, it is generally accepted that Tre'r Ceiri was occupied throughout Roman times, as the remains of rectangular buildings, built in stone, show a distinctive Roman influence.

Another Welsh hillfort, similar to Tre'r Ceiri, is Carn Fadryn (SH 278352). This fort's name is still spelt in various ways even in modern Welsh. It is a conical hill with a fortress at its summit. It retains its impressive stone ramparts and hut circles. Carn Fadryn also has a stone on its summit known as the Bwrdd y Brenin, or King's Table, which is supposed to conceal a pot of gold.

Left *Tre'r Ceiri, a Celtic settlement on the Lleyn Peninsula. It was occupied for several centuries*

Below *Carn Fadryn, an impressive and isolated hilltop settlement on the Lleyn Peninsula*

## ANGLESEY & THE MENAI STRAIT

THE ROMANS considered the Druids to be the greatest threat to conquest in the whole of the Celtic kingdoms, and so it became vital that their stronghold and 'university on Môn or Anglesey (SH 484624) be destroyed with all dispatch. The attack came in 60–61AD.

The Druids – probably both male and female, although there is some dispute on the existence of Druidesses – gathered on the opposing shore to howl down curses and imprecations on the heads of the detested Romans. Druids were exempt from military service, so it could be that they were unable to

*Above The Menai Strait between Caernarfon and Anglesey, forded by Roman attackers to destroy the Druids*

fight back; or perhaps their gods were as unfamiliar with Roman weaponry as the brave inhabitants of Maiden Castle in the West. Whatever the reason, the curses drowned in the Strait, and the Druids were thoroughly defeated, never to rise again on British soil. (It was a different story in Ireland, but that's a tale for another day). Their sacred groves were destroyed, and the priesthood was slaughtered.

## CAERWENT

THE SOUTH OF WALES received 3 'Caers' between 75 and 80 AD. The first was Venta Silurum (Caerwent, ST 469905), the tribal capital of the troublesome Silures. The town, which was walled in later centuries, was small but beautifully formed, with a forum, basilica, a temple and public baths. The main street ran east–west. The forum was a complex of town hall (the basilica), law courts, marketplace and council offices. Mosaics of the town houses have been found, though these are now lost. The ground plan of a Romano–Celtic temple is still visible near the church, showing the central shrine, outer wall and verandah. There are also some fine inscribed stones. An altar to the Celtic god Mars–Ocelus is now in the National Museum at Cardiff, along with one of the mosaics. Much of the town wall still stands, and the town street plan still preserves its 2000 year old pattern.

*Surviving Roman walls at Venta Silurum, now Caerwent, in south Wales*

## CAERLEON

ABOUT 16KM (10 miles) west of Caerwent, along what is now the A48, stands Isca Legionis (Caerleon, ST 339906), also known as Isca Silurum. The possible site of an Arthurian battle after the Roman withdrawal, its name means City of the Legion. It was the legionary fortress headquarters of the Legio II Augusta, who were responsible for most of the forward thrusts of the Roman army into Celtic areas. It was founded at around the same time as Caerwent. The best preserved aspect of Caerleon is its massive amphitheatre, built some five years after the fortress. It is oval in shape, 56m x 41.6m (184 x 136.5ft), and is the only amphitheatre to have been totally excavated in Britain. Estimates show that it would have seated about 6000 people, which was the approximate compliment of the occupying legion. It was probably used for parades, military exercises and weapons drill as well as for entertainments such as gladiator or animal fights. We cannot be certain how far the local population was involved in the amphitheatre's use; it may have been out of bounds for civilians not linked with the legion.

As a candidate for one of Arthur's 12 battles, that of the 'City of the Legion', there are neither records nor archaeological finds to substantiate the claim. Southern Wales was at this time becoming settled by the Irish, and it is possible that Arthur fought a battle with the encroaching Irish settlers. However, a preceding battle was at 'Cat Coit Celidon' or the Caledonian forest, north of

Below *The amphitheatre at Caerleon, south Wales, is the best preserved in Britain*

Right *Perhaps amphitheatres like these were the inspiration for the Round Table of Arthurian legend*

Hadrian's Wall. A retreat from there, or running skirmish down the western Roman road, might make Chester (Deva, SJ 405663) a contender for the battle. The enemy, in that case, would have been Pictish. Both Caerleon and Chester have surviving Roman amphitheatres, and the suggestion has been made that the famous Round Table of Arthur's court might, in fact, have been a circular meeting place. Any of the amphitheatres surviving in the decades after the Roman withdrawal might have served this purpose.

## CARMARTHEN

CONTINUING ALONG the A48, pass through Cardiff (Caerdydd ST 181766), which was a Roman foundation of the late 3rd/early 4th century and which houses the National Museum of Wales. Many finds from Romano–British Wales can be seen here. Onward through the south of the country to Moridunum (Carmarthen, SN 224120), another 'Caer' in the Romanised portion of Wales. The town and fort were only discovered in the late 1960s, and it is thought that Carmarthen was the tribal capital of the Demetae. The modern county name of Dyfed is the Welsh version of the tribal title. Carmarthen boasts an amphitheatre, although this is by no means as impressive as Caerleon's. Visible remains are limited to the mounds that formed the seating. Carmarthen's best claim to fame is probably that it became known as Merlin's town, and was thought to be the birthplace of Arthur's court wizard. A hill outside 'Caer Myrddin' is known as Merlin's Mount.

## CAERNARFON

FROM THE SOUTH to the north, and another Caer – this time Segontium (Caernarfon, SH 485624). It was from this auxiliary fort, built in 78AD, that the final assault was made on Mona (Anglesey), completing the work that had been done 18 years previously with the destruction of the Druids. After inflicting a dreadful defeat on the Ordovices, the tribe of the area, Anglesey completed the conquest of Welsh territory. It is said that the troops were forced to swim the Menai Strait, as no ships were available. The base at Segontium was garrisoned for at least 300 years. Remains can be seen of the commandant's house, the headquarters building and the strongroom where the legionary standards were kept. There is also evidence of a Mithraeum, Mithras being the soldiers' god. He was of Persian origin and his legend bears much similarity to that of Christ. A portion of Roman wall some 20ft high can still be seen about 150 yards west of the fort.

*Right Segontium, now Caernarfon, whose garrison was withdrawn to help Macsen Wledig claim the Roman Empire*

Above *The amphitheatre at Carmarthen, south Wales. The town claims to be the home of Merlin*

In 383AD, Macsen Wledig (Magnus Maximus) was declared emperor by the British troops. By this time, it must be pointed out, the majority of 'Roman' soldiers were recruited from the local population, and regardless of the legion's titles or origins, the legionaries would be British. Macsen was a local hero, and he withdrew the garrison of Segontium to help him in his bid for power. He failed, but Segontium was not garrisoned again.

## TOMEN–Y–MUR

AFTER THE COMPLETION of military conquest in Wales, many forts were built in strategic areas to consolidate Roman control over hostile natives. The most remote of these – probably the bleakest fort in Britain – was Tomen–y–Mur in Gwynedd (SH 707387). It is high in the mountains, 5m (8km) south of Ffestiniog. It was built in 78AD to typical plan (playing–card shaped) but reduced in size around 120AD. It had its own amphitheatre, which is the only one known to have been provided for an auxiliary fort. Presumably, the soldiers stationed there needed some diversion from the trials of their posting. The outlines of two practice camps can be seen, and despite its remoteness, a vicus (a civilian settlement which often grew up to supplement fort amenities) still existed outside the fort. The mound which is clearly visible in the fort plan is a Norman motte, showing that even 1000 years after Roman occupation, Tomen–y–Mur had strategic importance.

*Tomen-y-Mur, the bleakest Roman posting in Britain. Celtic resistance was strong in this area, and even the Normans built a castle here*

*Left Caer Gybi, Anglesey, is a church built inside a Roman fort*

## CAER GYBI

ON ANGLESEY (Holyhead, SH 246827) itself, the remains of a Roman fort can be seen in an unusual setting: the earthworks enclose the church and churchyard of St Gybi. Caer Gybi, as it is known, was a small fort 76.2m x 53.34 m (250 x 175ft), and probably dates to the early fourth century. The relatively late date – towards the end of the occupation – indicates that it was built to protect against 'barbarian' invaders. These were probably the Irish, who were a constant threat from the west at this time. Ireland was never threatened by Rome, and retained its Celtic Iron Age culture up to the Middle Ages. The fact that the church was built inside the ancient walls, some of which still stand up to 4.5m (15ft) high, could indicate one of two things: either there was a need for the church to have great protection against attack; or the fort was built on (or became) a focal site for pre–Christian religious worship. Such sites were frequently adapted for Christian use, because the spiritual association of the location was already strong.

## DIN LLIGWY

AGAIN ON FAR WESTERN ANGLESEY, we have the remains of Din Lligwy (SH 496862). This settlement, enclosed by a pentagonal wall, dates from the 3rd or 4th centuries (opinions differ depending on the source of information), late in the occupation. There are several rectangular buildings and two round huts in the enclosure, which is about 0.2ha (0.5acres) in area. Iron smelting is indicated by two hearths, and other finds show that Din Lligwy was the home of a British chieftain. They are rich in comparison to other native sites of the same period, and show a degree of acceptance of Roman lifestyle which is unusual in this part of Britain.

*Right Din Lligwy on Anglesey was the home of a British chieftain during Roman times*

## DINAS EMRYS

DINAS EMRYS (SH 606492) is a hillfort 1.6km (1mile) north east of Beddgelert, beside the A498. Here, Vortigern fled in the fifth century when his policy of paying Saxon mercenaries to defend northern and eastern Britain backfired, and the Saxons began to demand more land and payment. Eventually they became invaders themselves, much more determined than the Romans. Dinas Emrys seems to have been occupied before, during and after the Roman occupation, though not continuously, and is one of few British sites to claim this distinction. It was certainly re–occupied in Vortigern's time, and the objects found here suggest both wealth and the possibility of a Christian household. The level summit measures around 152.4m x 91.4m (500 x 300ft). The original entrance is in the west, with a steep climb through three ramparts. The easier approach is to the east.

*Dinas Emrys, north Wales, was the stronghold of Vortigern. He was responsible for the Anglo-Saxon invasions of Britain*

Right *Offa's Dyke, built by a Mercian king to separate the Welsh and the Saxons*

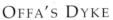

## OFFA'S DYKE

OFFA'S DYKE is a massive earthwork running virtually the entire length of the old Saxon/Welsh border, from the River Wye in the south to the Dee in the north. It marks the border between Wales and the Saxon kingdom of Mercia: parts of it still form the current Welsh/English border. The 'defensive' aspect of the Dyke – more symbolic than actual, for their are no fortifications or military encampments along its line – shows that it was probably built as a warning to the Welsh, with the ditch on its western side. 112.6km (70 miles) long and still standing 15.2m (50ft) high in places, it is an impressive testimony to the Mercian king who initiated its construction between 757 and 796.

*St Gybi's Well (Ffynon Gybi) on the Lleyn Peninsula, Wales*

## FFYNON GYBI

FFYNON GYBI, or St Gybi's Well (SH 429412) is just northeast of Pwllheli. It is said that Gybi came from Ireland with his uncle and a group of disciples in a large coracle, and were shipwrecked near here. St Gybi built a sanctuary, where he dwelt for many years. The well has been used both for healing and for divination, the latter mainly by young women. They would test the faithfulness of their lovers by casting a rag into the water and noting the direction in which it floated. There is a local legend linking St Gybi with the king Maelgwn Gwynedd, who was known as the 'Dragon of the Isle'. His stronghold was on Anglesey, and there is also a church dedicated to St Gybi on the island, built in the remains of a Roman fort.

## FFYNON BERIS

FFYNON BERIS, St Peris' Well (SH 609583) can be found by the A4086 near Old Llanberis. St Peris is, like so many of his contemporaries, something of a shadowy figure about whom little is known. The well is best known for being the home of a giant serpent or eel. It was said that it would heal anyone bathing there by coiling around them. Unfortunately, this compassionate creature did not take into account human frailty: a young girl died of fright when it coiled around her, presumably causing great distress to the serpent who was only trying to do its job. There has been a suggestion that, in the early days of Christianity, the well contained sacred fish, and this may be the basis for the legend.

*St Peris' Well (Ffynon Beris), Wales.*
*A serpent used to inhabit the waters*

## ST WINIFRED'S WELL

ST WINIFRED'S WELL (SJ 184764) in Holywell is one of the most visited holy wells in Britain. Gwenfrewi, as she is known in Welsh, spurned the advances of the Welsh prince Caradoc, and in a rage he struck off her head with his sword. A spring welled up where her head fell. Luckily, her uncle St Beuno was able to miraculously restore her to life, but he cursed Caradoc and his descendants. The only cure for their subsequent affliction was immersion in the well. Gwenfrewi, meanwhile, went on to become a most holy nun and died as Abbess of Gwytherin near Llanrwst. Her remains were moved – or translated, as the process is known – to Shrewsbury Abbey in 1138. The well is remarkably well maintained and is in the care of Roman Catholic nuns. The stones and moss at the bottom of the well are red–tinged and are said to be the hair and blood of Gwenfrewi.

Left *St Winifred's Well, Holywell, Wales. It is still a place of pilgrimage for thousands of people*

Right *St Govan's Chapel, Pembrokeshire, which may be the burial place of King Arthur's knight, Sir Gawain*

Far right *The altar and stone seat in St Govan's chapel are the oldest parts of the building*

## ST GOVAN'S HEAD AND CHAPEL

THIS REMOTE LITTLE CHAPEL on the south Pembrokeshire coast (SR 967930) typifies the needs of the early Celtic saints for solitude. It is reached by a precarious set of steps set into the cliff face, and these pass through the chapel and down to the sea. It is said that they cannot be counted, like the steps leading to the monastery ruins at Whitby in North Yorkshire. The fabric of the chapel, as it stands, is probably 13th century and measures 5.4m x 3.6m (18 x 12ft).

The surviving altar and a rock seat in the chapel, however, probably date back to the time of St Govan himself. His origins are, like many of his contemporaries, obscure. His name is said to be a corruption of Gawain, linking him to Arthurian legend, and St Govan's Head is one of several places suggested as Gawain's burial place. Listen carefully when visiting this picturesque site: a bell was supposedly hidden among the rocks by mermaids, who rescued it from pirates who had stolen it from the chapel.

## MAEN ACHWYFAN CROSS

THE MAEN ACHWYFAN CROSS (ST 129787) is not far from Holywell in Clwyd, and is set at a crossroads which may indicate the junction of ancient routes in Wales. It is one of the tallest wheel crosses in Wales, and bears a distinct resemblance to the Cornish crosses mentioned earlier. Like the crosses at Carew and Nevern (see below), all 4 sides of the supporting pillar are carved with interlace and geometric designs, as well as pictures. One panel is supposed to show a man treading on a serpent. This particular representation is a popular one in Christian iconography, usually thought to symbolise St George or St Michael killing the dragon. Dragons or serpents are often seen as a metaphor for paganism, therefore such carvings are usually thought to represent the triumph of Christianity over heathen worship.

*The Maen Achwyfan Cross, near Holywell, stands by an ancient road*

## CAREW CROSS

THE CAREW CROSS (SN 047037), one of the most famous in Wales, now stands beside the A4075 near the entrance to Carew Castle. The cross dates from the 6th century, and its carved designs include an interlace of one continuous looping ribbon and a swastika. Far from being an evil symbol, the swastika is one of the most ancient sun signs recognised in the world, promising good fortune. The inscription which can be seen on the cross is much newer than the monument itself, dating from the 10th century. It reads: MARGIT EUT. RE X. ETG FILIUS (King Mariteut son of Edgar). This particular king died in 1035, but the use of the Carew Cross for his memorial inscription shows the reverence in which the monument was still held after 500 years.

*The Carew Cross, south Wales, with its intricate Celtic knotwork designs*

## NEVERN

NEVERN (SN 082401), near Fishguard and St David's, has an amazing collection of Celtic Christian stones and inscriptions gathered in a very small area. The Pilgrim's Cross is the furthest from the village, on the road to Frongoch some 137m (150yds) from the church. A cross is cut in relief on the rock face, and below it is a place for kneeling in prayer marked with a second, incised cross. Nevern was on the pilgrimage

Left *The Pilgrim's Cross, outside Nevern in Wales, marks the site of an ancient wayside shrine*

Right *Another Celtic cross, this one in Nevern churchyard*

route between Holywell and St David's Cathedral, and this cross marks a wayside shrine on the route.

Nevern Church is dedicated to St Brynach, a rather prolific king who reputedly fathered more than 20 children, all of whom became saints. There are several Celtic monuments in and around the church. The carved cross in the churchyard is similar to the Carew Cross, standing 3.8m (12.5ft) high. All 4 sides are decorated with knotwork panels. Some inscriptions have been described as 'Scandinavian' in influence, but they have never been deciphered, which makes this definition doubtful. It is said that on St Brynach's Day, 7 April, the first cuckoo of spring lands on the cross and sings.

Inside the church, the visitor is well–advised to study the windowsills as well as the more usual aspects of church architecture. Inscribed stones from the local area, some dating from the 5th century, have been embedded there. One bears the inscription 'The monument of Maglocunus son of Clutarius' in both Latin and Ogham. Ogham is a

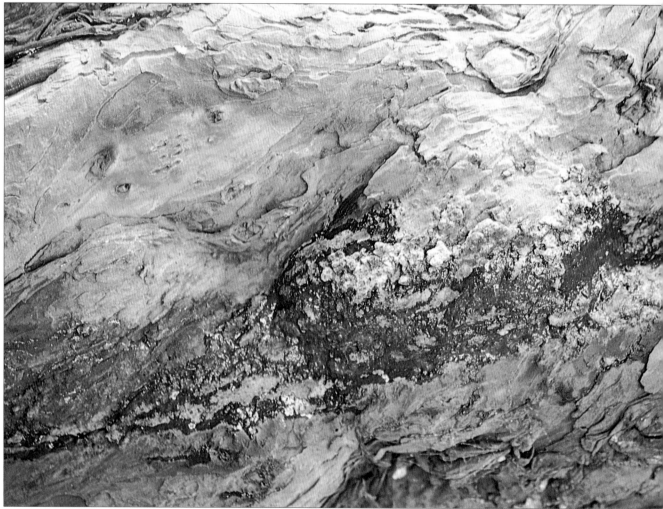

script of Irish origin which consists of lines scratched across the vertical edge of a stone, and it is the bilingual nature of these stones which allowed it to be deciphered. It also shows the close links between the Celtic church in Wales and Ireland.

Another inscribed stone in the church is an unusual inscribed cross. It is an interlace ribbon design and may have been used as an aid to prayer and meditation. By following the twists and turns of such patterns with the eye or a finger, a state of deep concentration akin to trance can be reached. Gazing patterns, as they are called, can be found world wide and date back thousands of years.

While visiting Nevern, it is also worth noting the Bleeding Yew Tree in the churchyard, which is said to be 700 years old and bleeds where an innocent man was hanged from the missing limb. Yew trees were sacred to the pre–Christian Celts and it is thought that their proliferation in churchyards is a continuation of belief in the tree's immortal nature. The stream which runs beside the church has also been described as holy, although there does not seem to be a well in the immediate vicinity.

Left *The sap runs red from the Bleeding Yew tree in Nevern churchyard*

Above *This cross, in relief, forms one of the windowsills in Nevern church*

*The inscription on this stone is written in Latin and Ogham. Ogham was a type of Irish writing said to be used by the Druids*

## BARDSEY ISLAND

Bardsey island (SH 120220) or Ynys Enlli is a tiny island (4.8km/3 miles in circumference) visible from the far western tip of the Lleyn Peninsula. This island is said to have once been joined to the mainland, and the sea between them is part of the lost, drowned land of doomed king Gwyddno Garanhir. The man responsible for the drowning was named Seithenin, and the medieval Welsh triads call him 'one of the three arrant drunkards of the Island of Britain'.

The monastery remains now visible on the island are those of the 13th century Augustinian priory of St Mary's, but the first monastery was supposedly founded by St Cadfan in 429. Since that time, more than 20000 saints are said to be buried here, and there are tales that so many bones have been dug up over the years, they have even been used as fenceposts. The enchanter Myrddin is also said to be buried here, where he guards the 13 Treasures of Britain.

*Bardsey Island, off the Lleyn Peninsula, burial place of 20000 saints*

## KILPECK CHURCH

NOT QUITE IN WALES, Kilpeck (Hereford & Worcester, SO 445305) near the Welsh border, is probably named for an Irish hermit. The present day church of Sts Mary and David is the successor of the early church, dating from the 12th century. The church is famous for its carvings, particularly those around the south door. They include human heads, fantastic beasts, and a 'green man' (a pagan woodland deity). Also at Kilpeck is one of the very few examples of a Sheela–na–gig carving outside of Ireland. Sheela–na–gigs are thought to represent a Celtic fertility goddess. All of the carvings at Kilpeck, despite their late date, are in a tradition unbroken since pre–Roman times, and illustrate pagan Celtic nature worship, fertility rites and the cult of the head.

*A Sheela-na-gig and Celtic head at Kilpeck church, Hereford & Worcester. The church is 12th century, but the carvings come from an ancient tradition*

## CASTELL CARREG CENNEN

NORMAN IN ORIGIN, the frontal wall of Carreg Cennen Castle (SN 667191) rises from a vertical cliff 91.4m (300ft) above the Cennen gorge. The Welsh prince Rhys ap Gruffydd captured the castle in the late 12th century during his campaign for Welsh independence, and was responsible for the extension of a 60.96m (200ft) cave through the mountain which houses a spring, now a wishing well. Carreg Cennen's position and its unique water supply made it an ideal base for Rhys' guerilla warfare against the despised English.

On the riverbank nearby is the cave of Ogof Dinas, which contains a rock shaped like a seated, cloaked figure. This is said to be Owain Lawgoch (Redhand), a 14th century Welsh hero who was poised to invade and free Wales with an army made up primarily of Welsh deserters from the troops of the Black Prince in France. Betrayed and murdered before his campaign could succeed, legend claims that his head was smuggled to Ogof Dinas. Here, like Arthur, he waits until Wales calls him. Carreg Cennen became such a powerful centre of resistance that the castle was dismantled in 1492 to make it useless as a stronghold.

Above *Castell Carreg Cennen, captured by Welsh Prince Rhys ap Gruffydd in his wars against the English*

Right *The castle was dismantled by the English to discourage Welsh resistance*

## 3. THE NORTH AND SCOTLAND

I HAVE INCLUDED northern English sites in this section, because it is only in relatively recent times that the border between the two lands has become fixed. The Scots (the name comes from 'Scotti', the Irish colonists who eventually became the dominant race in the years between the Romans and the Normans) have always been an ancient enemy of the English, and until 1707 when the parliaments of the two lands were united, the border shifted north and south depending on the fortunes of battle.

Scotland was populated by races much older than the Celts for thousands of years, and these may have been the forerunners of the Picts. It was not until about 300BC that the Iron Age appears to have reached here, 3 or 4 centuries later than in the south of Britain. The use of iron is held to be the point at which a place becomes defined as 'Celtic'. It is during this period that we see the building of duns, brochs and crannogs, and these are usually associated with the Celtic population of the north. Tribes known from this time include the Votadini, Selgovae and Novantae.

In around 80AD, Roman attention turned to northern Britain, and it was decided to extend the Roman frontier into Caledonia (Scotland). Garrisons were established in the north of Britain and two roads can be traced: one from Lancaster towards Glasgow, now submerged beneath the A6 and main rail line; and Dere Street, which led from Eboracum (York) into Scotland. The northern campaign culminated in a massive victory for the Roman legions at Mons Graupius, north of Inverness, in 84AD. Forts were built to deter Celtic uprising, but within 15 years every fort north of the line of Hadrian's Wall was violently destroyed. Tacitus, the Roman historian, records that 'Britain was conquered and at once abandoned'. It was 40 years before another attempt was made, culminating in the building of the Antonine Wall, but this, too, failed miserably. Caledonia and Britannia shared the land uneasily.

It was the Romans who named the 'Picti' or 'painted men' as being among the northern tribes. Whether they were pre–Celtic in origin is not known, but elements of their language suggest links with Iberia (Spain) and do not seem to be either Brythonic or Gaelic, the two Celtic strains of language. Their carved stones are among the most intricate and mysterious monuments of Celtic Britain. The Pictish and Irish ruling houses were joined in 843 with the accession of Kenneth Mac Alpin, and from this time that the land was known as Scotia.

*St Aidan, first bishop of Lindisfarne, who brought Celtic Christianity to Northumbria*

The Irish settlements in western Scotland paved the way for the advent of Christianity into Scotland, for St Columba was an Irish prince. His political power was as great as his spiritual, and it was due to his missionaries from Iona that Christianity spread throughout southern Scotland and northern England. Lindisfarne was an Irish foundation, and the monasteries of Jarrow and Monkwearmouth were its direct successors. The bishopric of Lindisfarne became the bishopric of Durham just prior to the Norman Conquest, and remains the third most powerful in the country.

Scotland's history in the centuries after 1066 is chequered. At times a client kingdom of the English, at others a mortal enemy, the desire for independence never died away. William Wallace died a traitor's death in 1305; Robert 1 (the Bruce) gained independence for the Scottish throne in 1328. A Scottish king came to the English throne in 1603, and in 1707 the Union was confirmed. The last true stand of the Celts, though it is doubtful whether they considered themselves as such, was at Culloden in 1746.

## CRANNOG (DUN TORCUILL)

CRANNOGS are artificial islands on which settlements were built. The word comes from the Gaelic 'crann', which means 'tree', and crannogs are most often to be found in Ireland and Scotland. There are some which have been found in Wales, most notably that which was studied by Channel 4's 'Time Team' in Brycheiniog. A crannog is, usually, an island platform raised on stilts in a lake, with buildings on top of the platform. Sometimes there is a bridge linking the platform with dry land, but often land could only be reached by boat. It is thought that crannogs were the fortified dwelling places of noble families, and that their position was primarily defensive. Most have now disappeared below water level, although there are some still visible as low–lying offshore islands. This crannog is at Dun Torcuill in Scotland. (NF 888737)

*Dun Torcuill, on North Uist in the Hebrides. It is a fortified dwelling built on a crannog*

## DUN TELVE, GURNESS AND MOUSA BROCHS

ANOTHER VERY SPECIFIC form of Celtic dwelling is the broch. These are round stone towers, and are found almost without exception only in the north and west of Scotland, particularly on the western isles. They are usually held to be the homesteads of Pictish people, and seem to have been 'fashionable' in the 1st centuries BC and AD. They are essentially two towers built one inside the other, with the rooms or galleries of the dwelling enclosed in the space between the walls. The inner courtyard formed by this circular structure was probably (though we don't know for certain) open to the sky, as some brochs have wells for catching rain–water in their courtyard. There is only a single entrance to these towers, often flanked by guard chambers.

Far left *The galleries inside the walls of Dun Telve broch, at Glenelg in Inverness*

Below *Buildings, perhaps of the Viking Age, inside the broch at Gurness on Orkney*

Dun Telve (NG 829173) in Inverness has a base 4.1m (13.5ft) thick at the entrance, and its inner courtyard is 9.75m (32ft) across. The wall survives to a height of about 10.2m (33.5ft).

The Broch of Gurness (HY 383267), on the Orkney mainland island, stands about 4.6m (15ft) high. The courtyard is 10.4m (34ft) across. After the broch fell out of use, later dwellers moved in and various new structures were built. Most are Celtic, but different styles show that the site was in use right up until Viking times.

The Broch of Mousa, on Shetland (HU 457236) is the largest, best preserved and most famous of all surviving brochs. Its dimensions also show it to have been rather larger and grander

than any of its contemporaries, although we have absolutely no idea of its owners' importance in the history of Celtic Scotland. It stands 13.1m (43.5ft) high yet has an internal diameter of only 6m (20ft). It is entered by a single door with guard chambers on either side. Timber ranges seem to have been built around the inside wall, supported above ground level. Timber galleries inside the walls are reached by uneven stairs, and the two towers are tied together with cross–stones.

Above *The broch of Mousa, in the Shetland Isles. Built in the Iron Age, it still stands over 31m (43ft) high*

## HADRIAN'S WALL

THE MARKER of the Roman Empire's northern frontier became known as Hadrian's Wall, named after the emperor who visited Britain in 122AD. It was built 'to separate the Romans from the barbarians', although it appears that the tribes immediately north of the wall had Roman sympathies and were not, at this time, a great threat. Forts were placed both north and south of the wall itself, usually within two miles of it, to help police uneasy areas. The wall eventually ran from Wallsend in the east to Bowness in the west, and great stretches of it still survive. In addition, the ground plans of many of its forts can still be seen.

Right *Hadrian's Wall at Walltown Craggs, Northumberland, built to control Celtic tribes*

## VINDOLANDA

ONE OF THE MOST IMPRESSIVE excavated sites, this one north of the wall, is Vindolanda (Chesterholm), near Bardon Mill in Northumbria (NY 357766). The most interesting remains are of the vicus, the civilian settlement which grew up around the fort to supplement the lifestyle of both soldier and local entrepreneur. A vicus generally contained bathhouses, inns, shops, markets and brothels as well as dwellings. Ordinary soldiers were not allowed to have their wives living in the fort, therefore they often dwelt in the vicus. On this site, we see how the native British combined their Celtic opportunism with Roman needs.

Vindolanda also has some excellent reconstructions on view, including an early wooden milecastle gate, stone turret, and lengths of wall both turf– and stone–built. Where possible, reconstructions of this type are carried out using original techniques, such as methods of dressing stone and mixes of mortar. Some parts are even built of the original stone, which had been pillaged in later years and has now been reclaimed. Designs are usually taken from better preserved examples, which can often be found in continental Europe. The excellent site museum has many finds from the site, including leather goods such as shoes which, in design, would not look out of place in a modern high street.

Left *Hypocaust pillars in the hot room of the military bath house at Vindolanda on Hadrian's Wall*

Above *A reconstructed Roman turret at Vindolanda, built using the original stones*

## CHESTERS

CHESTERS FORT (Cilurnum, NY 911700) is another extremely well–preserved site. One can see remains of the headquarters building, commandant's house with its hypocaust, and the military bathhouse. The hypocaust was the Roman central heating system, which provided underfloor heating through a system of flues and furnaces, and was highly efficient – as well as an absolute necessity in the northern climate of the time. The bathhouse, with its series of rooms and pools, is one of the best preserved in Britain. One can see the remains of the Roman bridge abutment across the river on which the fort stands; the bridge foundations are now on dry land, as the river has changed course in the last two millennia. The bridge is thought to have had three piers and to have supported a road 6m (20ft) wide.

Another fort worth visiting (not pictured) is Corbridge (NY 982648), which served as a supply base for the next northern campaign.

Left *The bridge abutments at Chesters Roman Fort on Hadrian's Wall*

Below *The bath house at Chesters, one of the best preserved in Britain*

## ANTONINE WALL

THE EMPEROR ANTONINUS Pius (138–161AD) decided that another attempt should be made to extend the northern frontier, and the result of this was the building of the so–called Antonine Wall, which commenced in 143AD. It stretched from the Forth to the Clyde rivers. Only two of its forts had stone walls, the rest being built of wood. The wall itself was turf built, and was never consolidated in stone. The wall could never be held: the independence of the tribes in this area had barely been touched by Roman influence and the invaders were driven out of the area within 15 years.

*A section of ditch marking the Antonine Wall, at Callendar House, near Falkirk, Scotland*

## ROUGHCASTLE

Above *At Roughcastle fort, on the Antonine Wall, these pits known as 'lilies' were dug as traps for attacking Celts*

THE BEST PRESERVED of the Antonine forts is Roughcastle (NS 843799), 9.6km (6 miles) west of Falkirk. It covers an area of approximately an acre, and ramparts and ditches can still be seen on three sides. Stone foundations of some interior buildings are still visible. The most important and unique aspect of the surviving remains is the existence of small defensive pits, called 'lilia' (lilies), 20 yards north of the defensive ditches. There are ten rows of these pit–traps, which would have had five sharpened stakes set point upwards in their base before being camouflaged with bracken and other vegetation. They were a deliberate trap for northern enemies, showing that despite the political assurances that the northern Celts were under control, they continued as a very real threat to Roman order.

Hadrian's Wall continued to be occupied right up to the end of the Roman occupation. In c.401AD, the emperor Honorius withdrew virtually all troops from Britannia in order to repel barbarian invasions on the continent.

Far right *Bamburgh Castle, Northumberland, built on the site of a British hillfort*

## BAMBURGH

BAMBURGH, (NU 184350) in Northumbria, seems a strange choice for a book on Celtic history, but as it has both British and Arthurian links it is worth mentioning. Best known as the fort of the Northumbrian Angle King Ida, and built as such in 547AD, it is a symbol of the relative ease with which the Germanic settlers integrated themselves into British life. No doubt, if there were documents surviving which could be authenticated as being contemporary with these settlements, we would have a better idea of British resistance other than that of the chieftains of Wales and the West Country. As it stands, however, our knowledge of the Northumbrian settlement comes from Bede, a Saxon monk writing a Saxon history – and it is well–known that history is written by the victors. Be that as it may, Bamburgh Castle is built on the foundations of a British promontory fort possibly known as Din Guayrdi, and was the model for the medieval 'Joyous Garde', the home of Sir Lancelot. Here he received the fugitive Tristan and Yseult, and here he brought Queen Guinevere after he rescued her from burning at Carlisle. The similarity of the British name is probably the reason for locating Lancelot here, although there may be a lost tradition of a northern British chieftain who was an ally of Arthur during the Saxon wars.

## PICTISH SYMBOL STONES

SOME INTRIGUING REMAINS from the Dark Ages come from Scotland. These are the so–called 'symbol stones' of the pre–Christian Picts. The designs on these stones include fantastic beasts, some of which are totally unrecognisable, and zigzag patterns which have no parallel in any other British culture. There are also Celtic knotwork designs, so there must have been some artistic influence between the two peoples. Later stones incorporate Christian imagery into their design,

Left *Strange Pictish symbols on a stone at Dunnichen, near Forfar (NO 508488)*

Right *Sueno's Stone (NJ 047595), east of Inverness. It shows a broch among its carvings*

probably coming from the Irish Celtic missionaries like Columba who were very active in Scotland from the fifth century onwards.

It is sometimes said that the Picts were, in fact, a loose confederation of strictly Celtic tribes which formed some time in the fourth century, but the Romans named them much earlier than this. Other evidence, mainly of placenames, suggests that their language had little in common with the Indo–European based British and Gaelic. The Picts (or Cruithne, as they called themselves) were eventually totally subsumed by the Irish (Scotti), in a way that the Romans, Anglo–Saxons and Normans were never able to do. Their language and culture was totally overtaken, in a few centuries, by the more powerful Irish. We are left with their carved stones and a few placenames.

*St Ninian's Church, at Whithorn in southern Scotland. It stands on the site of the first Christian community in Scotland*

## ST NINIAN'S CHURCH

IN THE EARLIEST DAYS of the Christian Church, perhaps even before the Roman occupation of Britain was officially at an end, a saint called Ninian established a community at Whithorn (NX 446403), in the southernmost county of modern Scotland. He is described as a Welshman who had been educated at the monastery of Tours, in France. The church of the community, unusually for the time, was built of stone which was painted or plastered white, making it a

strikingly visible building. It was therefore known as the Candida Casa, or White House. The community was a large one, and from here missionaries of the Celtic church travelled into northern Scotland, Wales, and are even recorded in Brittany. The existing chapel at Whithorn is much later than that of Ninian, but probably shares the site of the original.

## St Ninian's Cave

NINIAN PREFERRED SOLITUDE to community life, as was the wont of so many abbots and priests of the time. A cave to the west of Whithorn village (NX 423360), named for the saint, is still a place of pilgrimage. There are crosses carved into the rock and, occasionally, prayers or messages of thanks left there by modern day pilgrims. The view from the cave is only of the sea and sky, a most solitary place, perfect for the quiet reflections of a holy man who believed that closeness to God came only by denying the distraction of worldly pursuits and one's fellow man.

*St Ninian would retire to this cave for solitude. It is still a place of pilgrimage*

## IONA

I N THE YEAR 563, a century or more after Ninian, a band of exiles from Ireland landed in the Irish ruled kingdom of Ard–Gael (Argyll) in western Scotland. Their leader was Columba, a prince of the Ui Niall who were High Kings of Ireland. Styled a bishop, he and his followers established a community on the island of Iona (NM 284243). This became the main house of the Christian community of the north, and its strength lay not only in the fact that it was the base for great missionary work, but also in the great political power wielded by its abbot. The Irish were, at this time, steadily overcoming the native population, and Columba was in demand not only as a man of God, but as a representative of the Irish rulers as well. I find it fascinating, in light of Celtic history, that Columba referred to Christ as his 'Archdruid'.

The visible remains on Iona are all much later than Columba. His community lay westward of the present monastery, and his cell is marked by a mound. The hill of Dun I, the highest peak of the island, rises above it. The original Celtic settlement consisted of a large central cell, probably belonging to Columba himself, which was set a little apart from the

*The Bay of Coracles on Iona, where St Columba landed in the year 563*

others; and other cells set around it for the other monks. There was a communal church and other monastic buildings, including a refectory and scriptorium. The world famous Book of Kells, held to be a sublime representation of Celtic Christian art, was written on Iona. It was only taken to the monastery at Kells on the Irish mainland when Viking raiders threatened Iona in the 9th century.

Finally, the graveyard of Iona was already a sacred burial place before Columba's arrival. It has continued as such until the present day. Pictish, Irish and Scandinavian royalty rest here, carried from the Scottish mainland to lie in sacred soil. For them, Iona was the western isle in the sunset, in the Celtic Lands of the Blessed. Macbeth and Robert the Bruce are buried here. So is John Smith, the leader of the Labour Party who died in the early 1990s. It was his express wish that he be buried on the holy isle of his ancestors.

Top right *The remains of Columba's cell on Iona*

Bottom right *Iona, burial place of Celtic, Pictish and Scandinavian kings*

## LINDISFARNE

DURING THE EARLY 7th century, Edwin became King of Northumbria after a Saxon civil war, and the sons of the defeated king fled into exile. One of the sons, Oswald, spent several years of his exile on Iona. When he was returned to power, he asked Columba to send a bishop to found a monastery and bring Christianity to his kingdom. So in 630, Columba sent Aidan and some followers to the king, and they chose to establish their community on Lindisfarne (NU 125417). Even today, the island (known as Holy Island, though this name is much later than its foundation) can only be reached across a narrow causeway at low tide. The community was ascetic and strict in its regime, and bore little resemblance to the Benedictine foundations of the Middle Ages. Aidan was a true missionary bishop in the tradition of his wandering forebears in Wales and Cornwall, and it was due to his work and reputation that much of Northumbria was converted from paganism. He never travelled on horseback, and despite his secular power as representative of the Irish kingdoms and the friendship of kings, he was best remembered for his saintliness and miracle working.

Aidan died in 651, leaning against a timber post in Bamburgh, below the fortress of the king. In the modern day church of St Aidan in the town, there is still a shrine and votive light to his memory. It is said that a young shepherd near Melrose Abbey, another staunchly Celtic foundation, witnessed the miracle of a soul being lifted to heaven on a beam of light, accompanied by an angelic host. On learning that he had witnessed the glorious ascent of St Aidan, the shepherd decided to become a monk. His name was Cuthbert.

Between the death of Aidan and the appointment of Cuthbert as prior of Lindisfarne, the Celtic and Roman churches were reconciled – though this is a relative term. It meant that the British Christian Church now owed allegiance to Rome and all its liturgies and festivals were standardised, but legislation from the continent could not destroy centuries of Irish training. For St Cuthbert, the way to God lay through the renunciation of worldly life and the punishment and purification of his earthly body – in other words, he desired to become a hermit, solitary and remote from the community. In 676 he moved to one of the Farne islands, now a bird sanctuary, and built a cell there. It was only in 685, two years before his death, that he was persuaded (forced may be a better word) to leave his peaceful life and become Bishop of Lindisfarne.

*Right Lindisfarne Castle, built on the island where Christianity first came to Northumbria in AD630*

*Overleaf The ancient rainbow arch of Lindisfarne Priory, looking east*

## JARROW, MONKWEARMOUTH AND DURHAM

I WANT TO INCLUDE these three northern sites because, although they are Saxon rather than Celtic foundations, they owed their prosperity and existence to the legacy brought to the east of Britain by Aidan and the Celtic Church.

The monasteries at Jarrow (NZ 339652), on the River Tyne, and at Monkwearmouth (NZ 402578), north of Sunderland on the River Wear, were dedicated respectively to St Paul and St Peter. Although more than 10 miles apart, they were what became known as a twin community. Much of the masonry at Jarrow is Saxon, and one of the windows still has its original 7th century stained glass. The 'old' and 'new' churches – actually the chancel and the nave – are not truly joined together and several centuries separate the building of the two. The church was built in 681 on the site of a Roman temple. Jarrow's most famous son was the Venerable Bede, a historian without whose writings we would know nothing about this period of history.

St Peter's at Monkwearmouth was built at around the same

Left *The ruins of the monastery at Jarrow near Newcastle, home of the Saxon historian Bede*

Inset *the shrine of St Aidan in Bamburgh church, Northumberland*

time as Aidan was founding the community at Lindisfarne, so it is highly likely that its first incumbents taught in the Celtic tradition. The monastery which eventually grew up here was Bede's early home, and although his writings criticise the Celtic Church for their refusal to accept Roman rulings – particularly on the date of Easter – he was a great admirer of St Aidan. The church, surrounded on all sides by housing estates and industry, was severely damaged by fire a few years ago, but most of its exterior Saxon heritage is still visible.

Durham Cathedral (NZ 273421), the burial place of Bede and of St Cuthbert, is a magnificent Norman building which, with the medieval castle, dominates the city's high ground in a loop of the River Wear. It owes its very existence to that most ascetic of Celtic hermits, St Cuthbert. During the Viking invasions of the 9th century, Lindisfarne was attacked and many of the monks murdered. Some of the community fled inland, carrying with them the Island's holiest treasures: the relics of Cuthbert and the Lindisfarne Gospels. The Gospels show the height of Northumbrian art, a wonderful and still dazzling blend of Celtic, Saxon and continental illumination. The

*Durham Cathedral, founded in 995 to house the remains of St Cuthbert, hermit and Bishop of Lindisfarne*

interlace designs of this manuscript are the definitive version of Celtic knotwork, and could only have come from the imagination of monks who were familiar with the Irish Books of Kells and Durrow.

The monks of Lindisfarne (and their successors) stayed at Chester–le–Street in Co Durham for 100 years, then again decided to move on with their treasures. Through the auspices of a miracle, whereby the cart bearing Cuthbert's body refused to be moved while the travellers rested at a bend in the river Wear, it became clear that Dun–holme was to be the final resting place of the saint. His shrine is in the Chapel of the Nine Altars in the cathedral, but photographs of the interior are not permitted without prior permission of the Dean and Chapter. Durham Cathedral is a World Heritage site and much of the fabric is more than

*Left St Peter's church, Monkwearmouth near Sunderland. It was built in the 7th century*

*Right St Paul's Church at Jarrow. The chancel is 7th century, but the nave was built three centuries later*

# SELECTED BIBLIOGRAPHY

Ashe, G (ed), *The Quest for Arthur's Britain* Pall Mall Press, 1968

Ashe, G, *Traveller's Guide to Arthurian Britain* Gothic Image Publications, 1997

Barber, C, *Mysterious Wales* Granada, 1982.

Bord, J & C, *A Guide to Ancient Sites in Britain* Paladin, 1978

Bord, J & C, *Mysterious Britain* Paladin, 1974

Broadhurst, P, *Sacred Shrines* Pendragon Press, 1988

Clayton, P (ed), *A Companion to Roman Britain* Phaidon Press, 1980

Feachem, R, *Guide to Prehistoric Scotland* Batsford Press, 1977

Hogg, AHA, *A Guide to the Hillforts of Britain* Paladin, 1975

Laing, L, *Celtic Britain* Paladin, 1979

Mackie, JD, *A History of Scotland* Pelican, 1964

May, J, *Fogou*. Gothic Image Publications, 1996

Meyrick, J, *A Pilgrim's Guide to the Holy Wells of Cornwall* J Meyrick, 1982

Michell, J, *A Traveller's Guide to Sacred England* Gothic Image Publications, 1996

Stobie, D, *Exploring the Legends and Sites of King Arthur* Parkgate Books, 1998

Straffon, C, *Pagan Cornwall – Land of the Goddess* Meyn Mamvro Publications, 1993

Woolf, C, *Introduction to the Archaeology of Cornwall* Bradford Barton Ltd, 1970